/Word
Nerd

An Hachette UK Company
www.hachette.co.uk

First published in Great Britain in 2019 by Cassell, an imprint of
Octopus Publishing Group Ltd
Carmelite House
50 Victoria Embankment
London EC4Y 0DZ
www.octopusbooks.co.uk

Copyright © Susanna Geoghegan 2019

Distributed in the US by Hachette Book Group
1290 Avenue of the Americas
4th and 5th Floors
New York, NY 10104

Distributed in Canada by Canadian Manda Group
664 Annette St., Toronto, Ontario, Canada M6S 2C8

Text by Michael Powell
Design by Milestone Creative

ISBN 978 1 78840 201 9

A CIP catalogue record for this book is available from the
British Library.

Printed and bound in China

10 9 8 7 6 5 4 3 2 1

Introduction

English is full of beauty and surprises. If you're a lover of the weird and wonderful, from fascinating etymology to the ten most overused and useless English phrases, it's time to get your nerd on.

Get the inside dope on a wealth of curiosities hiding in plain sight within the English language. You'll discover the correct name for the dot over the letter 'i'; the English word for *Schadenfreude*; the collective noun for a group of seagulls; the Bechdel test; the opposite of serendipity; lots of words and phrases invented by Shakespeare; the anatomical name for your big toe and the only word in the English language that contains five consecutive vowels.

Despite its pellucid antiprolixity, this book isn't averse to a peppering of persiflage. It garners a smorgasbord of amuse-bouches vis-à-vis the English language, which is always cromulent but rarely misses an opportunity to metagrobolize!

A **logolept** is another term for a word nerd.

Achluophobia is the fear of darkness.

Epeolatry: (n)
the <u>worship</u> of words

What's the difference between a **bibliophile** and a **bibliophagist?**

Acrophobia is the fear of heights.

A bibliophile loves the look, the smell and the aesthetic of books, and may have hundreds of them displayed proudly at home – including several first editions – and may even boast excitedly about loving books. The bibliophagist is the real deal because he or she is simply a voracious reader. Which one are you?

An army of bloodhounds

Invented by science fiction:

Robot

First used in Karel Čapek's 1920 Czech play R.U.R. ('Rossum's Universal Robots') to refer to factory-made artificial humans.

The origin of the meaning of the word **'chaperone'** as someone who accompanies or supervises another is a metaphor, because a chaperon was a hood formerly worn by nobles.

Alektorophobia is the fear of chickens.

There's a word for that:

Screenager A young person who spends a lot of time watching television or using digital technology, such as a computer or smartphone.

Philothaumaturge Someone who loves magic.

Rasceta The creases in the skin on the inside of your wrists.

Sophrosyne An ancient Greek concept of excellence of character and soundness of mind, characterized by self-control, moderation, temperance; the antonym of hubris.

Interesting eponyms

Sideburns

were originally called 'burnsides', named after Union Army General and United States Senator Ambrose Burnside (1824–81), who was noted for his unusual facial hair.

Spelunking is the hobby of cave exploration, from spêlunx, the ancient Greek word for cave or cavern.

The earliest written example lexicographers have of the adjective 'bitchy' is from a 1908 letter written by Virginia Woolf.

The word **'sport'**, comes from the Old French desporter, meaning 'to take pleasure'. Words such as 'athlete', 'pentathlon' and 'triathlon' come from the ancient Greek verb **athlein**, to compete for a prize.

Anatidaephobia is the fear of ducks.

A band of gorillas

The longest English word that can be spelled without repeating any letters is **uncopyrightable.**

Bumblebees were nicknamed 'foggy-toddlers' in the Scots dialect of the eighteenth century.

Ough: We pronounce the combination 'o-u-g-h' in nine different ways. This sentence contains them all: 'A rough-coated, dough-faced, thoughtful ploughman strode through the streets of Scarborough; after falling into a slough, he coughed and hiccoughed.'

Quake-buttock:
(n) a coward

Ask Dr Johnson:

The full title of Dr Samuel Johnson's ground-breaking diary published in 1755 is **'A dictionary of the English Language: in which the words are deduced from their originals, and illustrated in their different significations by examples from the best writers. To which are prefixed, a history of the language, and an English grammar'.** It defined over 42,000 words and took him eight years to compile, with six poorly paid copyists, for which he was paid 1,500 guineas, a small fortune even by today's money.

Arachnophobia is the fear of spiders.

There's a word for that:

Anagapesis The feeling of no longer loving someone or something once loved.

Jubate Having a mane.

Thalassiarch Someone who rules over the sea.

Pejorism The belief that the world is becoming worse.

A convocation of eagles

In the late seventeenth century, a hundred years before the eponymous ovoid nursery rhyme appeared, Humpty Dumpty was the name of a drink consisting of boiled ale and brandy.

A nodgecomb is a sixteenth-century word for a fool or simpleton.

Athazagoraphobia is the fear of being forgotten or not remembering things.

Whatever the weather:

Snell

Used to describe bitingly grim weather (especially the wind) that you can feel right down into your bones.

A parliament of owls

Sesquipedalian means long and ponderous (of words and expressions), or using long words, literally words 'a foot-and-a-half long'. In the eighteenth century, a **word-grubber** was a slang word for a sesquipedalian speaker or writer.

'**Go!**' is the shortest grammatically correct sentence in English.

Ask Dr Johnson:

Dr Samuel Johnson's diary contains dozens of humorously subjective entries, such as:

Oats

'**a grain, which in England is generally given to horses, but in Scotland supports the people**'.

Autophobia is the fear of abandonment.

<u>Invented by science fiction:</u>
Clone
In 1903, Herbert Webber – a plant physiologist at the United States Department of Agriculture – created the word 'clon' (from the Greek word for twig – <u>klon</u>) to describe the cutting taken from a plant. However, the word 'clone' wasn't applied to humans until it appeared in the best-selling book <u>Future Shock</u> in 1970, written by Alvin and Heidi Toffler. The 1932 dystopian novel <u>Brave New World</u> famously features human cloning (Bokanovsky's Process), but author Aldous Huxley never used the word 'clone' or 'cloning'.

Interesting eponyms

Many people are aware that **sadism** was named after the Marquis de Sade, but the origin of the eponym

masochism,

sexual pleasure in being hurt or abused, is less well-known. The term was invented by German neurologist Richard von Krafft-Ebing in reference to a heavily autobiographical novella by Leopold von Sacher-Masoch (1836–95) called <u>Venus in Furs</u>, about a man's sexual fascination with cruel, dominant women. (It is also one of the tracks on The Velvet Underground's 1967 debut album, <u>The Velvet Underground & Nico</u>.)

Avocado actually comes from a word meaning 'testicle'. When the Aztecs discovered the avocado in 500 BC, they probably noted its shape, size, gnarly skin and tendency to grow in pairs, and named it <u>āhuacatl</u>, which means 'testicle'. However, it is an urban myth that guacamole translates as 'testicle sauce'.

<u>**Barophobia**</u> is the fear of gravity.

A rookery of albatrosses

An enneacontakaienneagon **is a shape with 99 sides.**

Underground is the only word in the English language that begins and ends with **'und'**.

Ask Dr Johnson:

Excise

'A hateful tax levied upon commodities, and adjudged not by the common judges of property but wretches hired by those to whom excise is paid.'

There's a word for that:

Hypobulia The inability to make decisions.

Anepronym A trade name that has become a generic term for the item, such as Hoover, Jacuzzi or Aspirin.

Agastopia A rare condition in which an individual has love for a particular part of the body, and may favour using it or stop using it completely to keep it protected.

Uhtceare Lying awake before dawn worrying.

Bathophobia is the fear of depths.

J K Rowling invented the term 'Muggle' to refer to those in the Harry Potter universe who don't practise magic, but the word has been around for centuries. It first appeared in the thirteenth century in the epic poem <u>Brut</u> written by the poet Layamon, in which a muggle was 'a tail resembling that of a fish'. Then, in the early seventeenth century, the playwright Thomas Middleton used the word 'muggle' with the meaning of 'sweetheart' or 'wife': 'Oh the parting of us twain, Hath caus'd me mickle pain!, And I shall ne'er be married, Until I see my muggle again.' Then, in the 1920s, 'muggle' became slang for a cannabis joint, and in 1928, Louis Armstrong named one of his songs 'Muggles'.

Whatever the weather:
Watergaw

A lone patch of rainbow in the sky, but not a full rainbow. It is the subject of Hugh MacDiarmid's poem 'The Watergaw': 'a watergaw wi' its chitterin' licht ayont the on-ding'. The word **'iridule'** is similar and refers to a small rainbow-coloured patch of sky.

The first written example of **'chicken'** meaning **'coward'** appears in Will Kemp's <u>Nine Days Wonder</u> in 1600: 'It did him good to have ill words of a hoddy doddy! a hebber de hoy!, a chicken! a squib.'

<u>**Cacophobia**</u> **is the fear of ugliness.**

Semordnilap (aka heteropalindrome or anadrome) is a word or phrase that spells a different word or phrase backwards (semordnilap spells palindromes backwards), e.g. dog, plug, reviled, desserts, deliver no evil.

Boffering **is the hobby of engaging in mock medieval combat wearing padded armour and wielding a foam-covered weapon.**

A roll of armadillos

A monepic sentence is formed of a single word: 'Great!', 'Thanks', 'Awesome!', 'Hello'.

The longest one-syllable word in the English language is 'screeched'.

<u>Invented by science fiction:</u>

Gas giant

James Blish introduced the term in his story 'Solar Plexus' which was published in the anthology Beyond Human Ken in 1952.

<u>Catoptrophobia</u> is the fear of mirrors.

There's a word for that:

Zedonk The hybrid offspring of a zebra and a donkey.

Hemicacous Only half bad.

Grinagog Someone who appears to smile constantly, or for no apparent reason.

Ecdysis The process of shedding the old skin (in reptiles) or casting off the outer cuticle (in insects and other arthropods).

Ask Dr Johnson:

Stoat
'A small, stinking animal.'

A rasp of guinea fowl

To **scan** originally meant to 'study closely'.

Interesting eponyms

The origin of the eponym

quisling

– a traitor who collaborates with an enemy occupying force – is Vidkun Quisling, the Norwegian politician who headed the collaborationist regime during Norway's Nazi occupation. The Times newspaper helped to popularize the term with its editorial on 19 April 1940 entitled 'Quislings everywhere', which declared 'to writers, the word Quisling is a gift from the gods. If they had been ordered to invent a new word for traitor ... they could hardly have hit upon a more brilliant combination of letters.'

Chronomentrophobia is the fear of clocks.

Twenty common eggcorns

Coined by linguist Geoffrey Pullum in 2003, an eggcorn (which is itself an eggcorn of 'acorn') is an informal term for a word or phrase that is used in error, usually because it is a homophone (same sound with a different meaning) or sounds similar to the original word or phrase. How many eggcorns do you use?

1. Pacific/pacifically (specific/specifically)

2. Escape goat (scapegoat)

3. One foul swoop (one fell swoop)

4. Damp squid (damp squib)

5. On tender hooks (on tenterhooks)

6. All intensive purposes (all intents and purposes)

7. Pass mustard (pass muster)

8. Expresso (espresso)

9. Wet your appetite (whet your appetite)

10. Curve your enthusiasm (curb your enthusiasm)

11. Card shark (card sharp)

12. Doggy dog world (dog-eat-dog world)

13. Klu Klux Klan (Ku Klux Klan)

14. Present company accepted (present company excepted)

15. Prevaricate (procrastinate)

16. Shouldn't of (shouldn't have)

17. Tie me over (tide me over)

18. Unchartered territory (uncharted territory)

19. Worse case scenario (worst-case scenario)

20. Chomping at the bit (champing at the bit)

Dreamt is the only word in English that ends with 'mt'.

What is the difference between the mythical creatures hippalektryon **and** hippogryph**?**

A hippalektryon has the head, shoulders and forelegs of a horse and the wings, tail and legs of a cockerel; a hippogryph has the back half of a horse and the front half of an eagle.

Chronophobia is the fear of the future.

Numismatics is the hobby of collecting and studying money, but the term is most often associated with coins.

96 of the 100 most common English words have Germanic roots, and just those words make up more than half of all English used today.

Ostranenie:

(n) Artistic technique of making people see common things as strange or unfamiliar in order to force them outside of the usual patterns of perception.

A coalition of cheetahs

There's a word for that:

Skyme An old Yorkshire term meaning to 'glance sideways scornfully'.

Hypomnestic Having a very poor memory.

Malneirophrenia A foul mood resulting from a bad night's sleep.

Crambazzled An old Yorkshire term for looking prematurely aged through an excessive lifestyle such as drinking, drugs, partying, etc.

Coulrophobia is the fear of clowns.

A **pangram sentence** contains every letter in the language at least once. Here are five of them:

1. The quick brown fox jumps over a lazy dog.

2. Jived fox nymph grabs quick waltz.

3. Pack my box with five dozen liquor jugs.

4. How vexingly quick daft zebras jump.

5. The five boxing wizards jump quickly.

A **myriad** is literally 10,000 of something.

A self-enumerating pangram is a sentence that inventories its own letters, each of which occurs at least once. The first example was produced in Dutch by journalist Rudy Kousbroek, who then challenged British recreational mathematician Lee Sallows to create an English version. Sallows built an electronic 'pangram machine' which identified this solution: 'This pangram contains four As, one B, two Cs, one D, thirty Es, six Fs, five Gs, seven Hs, eleven Is, one J, one K, two Ls, two Ms, eighteen Ns, fifteen Os, two Ps, one Q, five Rs, twenty-seven Ss, eighteen Ts, two Us, seven Vs, eight Ws, two Xs, three Ys, & one Z.'

Ask Dr Johnson:

Bum

'The part on which we sit.'

Cryophobia is the fear of ice or cold.

A battery of barracudas

Whatever the weather:

Stoating

A Scots word for when it rains so heavily that the drops of rain bounce off the floor.

Ten famous mondegreens

A mondegreen is an eggcorn word or phrase
that appears in songs or verse.

1. 'Every time you go away,
   you take a piece of meat
   with you', **Paul Young**,
   'Every Time You Go Away'

2. 'Starin' at my momma's
   corpse, the summer'd
   seem to last forever',
   Bryan Adams, 'Summer
   Of '69'

3. 'Excuse me while I kiss
   this guy', **Jimi Hendrix**,
   'Purple Haze'

4. 'There's a bathroom
   on the right',
   **Creedence Clearwater
   Revival**, 'Bad Moon
   Rising'

5. 'I can see Deidre now,
   Lorraine has gone',
   Johnny Nash, 'I Can
   See Clearly Now'

6. 'We built this city on
   sausage rolls', **Starship**,
   'We Built This City'

7. 'I want a piece of bacon',
   The Ramones,
   'I Wanna Be Sedated'

8. 'Or should I just keep
   chasing penguins',
   Adele,
   'Chasing Pavements'

9. 'Hit me with your pet
   shark', **Pat Benatar**,
   'Hit Me With Your
   Best Shot'

10. 'A year has gone since
    I broke my nose', **The
    Police**, 'Message In
    A Bottle'

Cynophobia is the fear of dogs.

A siege of cranes

Queueing is the only word in the English language that contains five consecutive vowels.

Ask Dr Johnson:

Distiller

'One who makes and sells pernicious and inflammatory spirits.'

The expression 'dark horse' – meaning a little-known participant or underdog who achieves unprecedented success – was seeded in to the lexicon by Benjamin Disraeli in his 1831 novel <u>The Young Duke</u> in which he described a literal dark horse: 'A dark horse, which had never been thought of … rushed past the grandstand in a sweeping triumph.'

<u>Invented by science fiction:</u>

Computer virus

In 1970, American science fiction author and astrophysicist Gregory Benford published 'The Scarred Man', a story about a destructive computer program named VIRUS.

<u>Deipnophobia</u> is the fear of dinner parties.

There's a word for that:

Querencia From the Spanish verb <u>querer</u> (to desire); in bullfighting it is an area in the arena taken by the bull for a defensive stand; more widely, it is a place where one feels most at home, powerful, authentic. 'A querencia is a place the bull naturally wants to go to in the ring, a preferred locality … In this place, he feels that he has his back against the wall and … he is inestimably more dangerous and almost impossible to kill.' Ernest Hemingway, <u>Death in the Afternoon</u>

Whatever the weather:

Haboob

From the Arabic <u>habb</u>, meaning 'wind' or 'to blow', a haboob is a giant wall of dust or sand that usually occurs during the stormy summer months from a collapsing thunderstorm.

Interesting eponyms

Diesel fuel

is named after Rudolf Diesel (1858–1913), the French-born German engineer who invented the diesel engine.

<u>Dendrophobia</u> is the fear of trees.

What is the Bechdel test?

It is a measure of the representation of women in fiction (films, books, plays, etc.) A work passes the test if it features at least two women who talk to each other about something other than a man.

Tyrosemiophilia is the hobby of collecting cheese labels. People who practise the hobby are called 'tyrosemiophiles'.

A smack of jellyfish

English is the official language **of 67 countries and 27 non-sovereign nations, and is the** second most-spoken language **after Mandarin, with over 840 million users as a first or second language.**

<u>Ask Dr Johnson</u>:

Trolmydames

'Of this word I know not the meaning.'

<u>**Dentophobia**</u> is the fear of dentists.

There's a word for that:

Belvedere An open-sided gallery or a raised structure at the top of a house or on a vantage point, offering fine views of the scenery.

Oxter The hollow where the arm meets the shoulder (aka armpit).

Lunula The crescent-shaped, whitish area at the base of your fingernail.

Hippocrepiform Shaped like a horseshoe.

Tantle To keep busy without actually achieving anything.

Poecilonym is a synonym for the word 'synonym'.

The following sentence contains seven different spellings of the sound 'ee': **'He believed Caesar could see people seizing the seas.'**

The original meaning of **skullduggery** can be traced back to an old Scots legal term for a 'breach of chastity'.

<u>Dystychiphobia</u> is the fear of accidents.

A wake of vultures

(when feeding)

Interesting eponyms

The origin of the eponym

leotard

– tights worn for dancing – is Jules Léotard (1838–70), French acrobatic performer, trapeze pioneer and one-piece knitted garment wearer. He was the inspiration for George Leybourne's 1867 music hall song 'The Daring Young Man on the Flying Trapeze' but died three years later of smallpox, aged 32.

There's a word for that:

Queach A dense growth of bushes; a thicket.

Sprauchle Scots dialect word meaning to struggle to stand from an awkward seated position.

Accismus Coyly feigning disinterest in something that you really desire.

Mogshade Old English dialect word for the shadows cast by trees.

Ephebiphobia is the fear of teenagers.

<u>**Whatever the weather:**</u>

Dreich

A Scots word meaning
wet, dreary, miserable.

Approximately 4,000
new words **are added
to the English language
every year. That's about**
one every two hours.

A bask of crocodiles

Ten words Shakespeare 'invented'

1. Arch-villain <u>Timon of Athens</u>

2. Bloodstained <u>Henry IV Part I</u>

3. To elbow <u>King Lear</u>

4. Green-eyed (to describe jealousy) <u>The Merchant of Venice</u>

5. To swagger <u>A Midsummer Night's Dream</u>

6. Tardiness (as a noun) <u>King Lear</u>

7. Time-honoured <u>Richard II</u>

8. Unearthly <u>The Winter's Tale</u>

9. Unreal <u>Macbeth</u>

10. Zany <u>Love's Labour's Lost</u>

<u>Ergophobia</u> is the fear of work.

Invented by science fiction:

Alien

The first use of 'alien' for extraterrestrial beings is Philip Barshofsky's 1934 story 'One Prehistoric Night', which refers to Martians as aliens.

Linguists estimate that in Shakespeare's time, the English language contained only about **60,000 words** and that he probably knew nearly all of them. **Today there are about 180,000 words** plus about 50,000 obsolete ones. Shakespeare remains one of the greatest innovators of the English language ever to have lived. **He 'invented' more than 1,700 common words,** either by being the first to use a word in written language, devising a completely new word, combining existing words, adding prefixes and suffixes or being the first to use a particular noun as a verb or a verb as an adjective.

Ask Dr Johnson:

Stockjobber

'A low wretch who gets money by buying and selling shares.'

A flight of swallows

The dot over the letter 'i' is called a tittle.

Bumfiddle means to spoil a piece of paper or document.

Ask Dr Johnson:
Pissburnt
'Stained with urine.'

Genuphobia is the fear of knees.

There are only **four words** in the English language that end in **'-dous'** – tremendous, **horrendous,** stupendous **and hazardous.**

Since roughly only one out of every four users of English in the world is a native speaker of the language, most interactions in English take place among 'non-native' speakers.

A stand, or flamboyance of flamingos

Honorificabilitudinitatibus is the longest word in Shakespeare's works, and also the longest word in the English language featuring alternating consonants and vowels. It means 'the state of being able to achieve honours' **and appears in Act V, Scene I of <u>Love's Labour's Lost</u>. It is an example of a** hapax legomenon, **a word that occurs only once within a single text, author's opus or in the written record of an entire language.**

<u>Hippopotomonstrosesquippedaliophobia</u>

is the fear of long words.

There's a word for that:

Popliteal fossa Lozenge-shaped space at the back of the knee joint – the kneepit.

Ambisinistrous Equally clumsy with both hands, the opposite of 'ambidextrous'.

Paper hanger In US slang, someone who passes forged or fraudulent cheques.

Dactylonymy Counting using one's fingers.

Whatever the weather:

Twirlblast

An old English word meaning 'tornado'.

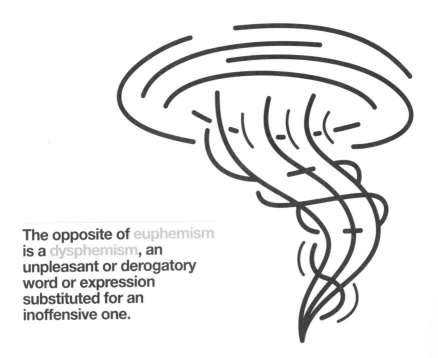

The opposite of euphemism **is a** dysphemism**, an unpleasant or derogatory word or expression substituted for an inoffensive one.**

Katsaridaphobia is the fear of cockroaches.

Lorem ipsum

The standard form of jumbled Latin text that is used by **typesetters and graphic designers** to demonstrate the textual layout of a document before the final text is available is called **'Lorem ipsum'**, and jumbled type has been used like this since the sixteenth century.

Don't let anyone convince you that English has no word for *Schadenfreude* **(taking pleasure from learning of or witnessing the misfortunes of another).** Epicaricacy **is a rare English word, from the ancient Greek** epikhairekakía**, 'joy upon evil'. It has rarely been used and has only recently been rediscovered by twenty-first-century lexicographers, although it does appear in some early dictionaries.**

There's a word for that:

Jakes To walk mud into a house (old English dialect word).

Walkative Inclined to walk; characterized by walking.

Phosphenes The stars and colours you see when you rub your eyes.

Pinna The mainly cartilaginous projecting portion of the external ear.

Kinemortophobia is the fear of zombies.

A mews of capons

A bookery is another name for a library, and its earliest written use was in 1798.

The correct name for the hashtag symbol is an octothorp.

#

Ask Dr Johnson:

Tarantula

'An insect whose bite is only cured by music.'

Interesting eponyms

The origin of the eponym

chauvinism

– fanatical patriotism, excessive or prejudiced support for one's own cause, group or sex – is Nicolas Chauvin, a possibly apocryphal French soldier who was wounded and disfigured 17 times because of his stubborn loyalty to Napoleon, and who became a figure of ridicule in Restoration France long after Napoleon's defeat.

Thrasonical:
Boastful.

Quidnunc:
A gossip or nosy person (Latin: 'what now?').

Koumpounophobia is the fear of buttons.

There's a word for that:

Sphallolalia Flirtatious talk that leads nowhere.

Lypophrenia A vague feeling of sadness, seemingly without any cause.

Anthimeria Using one part of speech as another part of speech, such as a noun as a verb or a verb as an adjective.

Acnestis The part of the back between the shoulder blades and the loins that you can't quite reach to scratch; derived from the Greek word for 'cheese-grater'.

Invented by science fiction:

Cyberspace

The word first appeared in a 1982 short story 'Burning Chrome' by American-Canadian cyberpunk author William Gibson.

Habitual nose picking is called **'rhinotillexomania'**.

The word 'noon' originally meant 3pm.

Mageirocophobia is the fear of cooking.

A bellowing of bullfinches

Whatever the weather:

Frazil

Frazil ice consists of loose, randomly oriented needle-like ice crystals formed in supercooled turbulent water, seeded by impurities in the water or grains of snow on the ocean surface. It is similar to the ice you get from a slush machine.

What is a contronym?

Single words that have two contradictory meanings (they are their own opposites) are known as contronyms, and they are quite rare. Here are ten of them:

1. **apology:** a statement of contrition for an action, or a defence of one

2. **bolt:** to secure, or to flee

3. **bound:** heading to a destination, or restrained from movement

4. **cleave:** to adhere, or to separate

5. **dust:** to add fine particles, or to remove them

6. **fast:** quick, or stuck or made stable

7. **left:** remained, or departed

8. **peer:** a person of the nobility, or an equal

9. **sanction:** to approve, or to boycott

10. **weather:** to withstand, or to wear away

Mysophobia is the fear of germs (aka **germophobia** or **bacterophobia**).

Metanoia:

(n) A change in one's way of life resulting from penitence or spiritual conversion.

Invented by science fiction:

Warp speed

Created by the writers of the original Star Trek television series.

Ask Dr Johnson:

Lizard

'An animal resembling a serpent, with legs added to it.'

Ten phrases Shakespeare 'invented'

1. A laughing stock,
   The Merry Wives of Windsor

2. All that glitters is not gold,
   The Merchant of Venice

3. As good luck would have it,
   The Merry Wives of Windsor

4. Break the ice,
   The Taming of the Shrew

5. Clothes make the man, Hamlet

6. Fair play, The Tempest

7. Forever and a day, As You Like It

8. Good riddance, Troilus and Cressida

9. Green-eyed monster, Othello

10. Heart of gold, Henry V

Nephophobia is the fear of clouds.

There's a word for that:

Antigropelos Coverings to protect the legs against wet mud.

Calodaemon A good or beneficial monster.

Pisculent Full of fish; that may be fished. (Obsolete, rare)

Demonachize To remove or drive monks permanently from (a place).

A squabble of seagulls

The word 'nice' – derived from Latin <u>nescius</u>, meaning 'ignorant' – began life in the fourteenth century when it meant 'foolish' or 'silly'. The word also attracted connotations of cowardice and sloth. It then came to mean 'shy' or 'reserved', and by the eighteenth century, it was associated with values of respectability and virtue.

<u>Ask Dr Johnson:</u>

Lunch

'As much food as one's hand can hold.'

<u>Nosocomephobia</u> is the fear of hospitals.

A panchreston is an explanation or argument that tackles a complex problem so broadly that it becomes meaningless.

During the sixteenth century, the word 'bully' was a unisex term of endearment that meant 'good fellow' or 'darling'. It later came to mean someone who showed off their good deeds, before finally acquiring its modern meaning.

Interesting eponyms

Shrapnel

was named after Henry Shrapnel (1761–1842), a lieutenant in the Royal Artillery during the Peninsular War who invented a type of fragmenting shell.

There's a word for that:

Gnathion The lowest point of the jawbone, and so the most outward pointing part of the chin.

Anemotropism Change in the growth or shape of an organism because of the wind.

Apotropaic Something that protects against misfortune and evil influences.

Pareidolia Seeing faces and images where none actually exists, for example the Virgin Mary in a grilled cheese sandwich.

<u>Octophobia</u> is the fear of the figure 8.

The literal meaning of bamboozle is 'to make a baboon out of someone'.

Pilots and air traffic controllers at major international airports have to speak English.

Deltiology is the hobby of collecting postcards.

Sphenopalatine ganglioneuralgia is the proper name for an ice-cream headache.

Silent letters, like the 'k' in 'knee' or the second 'b' in 'bomb', are called aphthongs.

Omphalophobia is the fear of belly buttons.

A gulp of cormorants

Whatever the weather:

Petrichor

The earthy smell produced when rain falls on dry soil. The word is formed from Greek <u>petra</u> ('stone') and <u>īchōr</u> (the fluid that flowed in the veins of the mythological Greek gods).

Ask Dr Johnson:

Sock

'Something put between the foot and shoe.'

Ten of Mrs Malaprop's malapropisms

A malapropism is like an eggcorn, but the substituted word or words are much wider of the mark, often turning the meaning into nonsense. They are named after Mrs Malaprop, a character in Richard Brinsley Sheridan's The Rivals (1775) who frequently makes this mistake.

1. He is the very pineapple of politeness!

2. If ever you betray what you are entrusted with … you forfeit my malevolence forever.

3. I am sorry to say, Sir Anthony, that my affluence over my niece is very small.

4. Oh! It gives me the hydrostatics to such a degree.

5. Why, murder's the matter! Slaughter's the matter! Killing's the matter! – but he can tell you the perpendiculars.

6. Nay, no delusions to the past – Lydia is convinced.

7. His physiognomy [is] so grammatical!

8. I am sorry to say, she seems resolved to decline every particle that I enjoin her.

9. Sure, if I reprehend anything in this world it is the use of my oracular tongue, and a nice derangement of epitaphs!

10. … she's as headstrong as an allegory on the banks of Nile.

Ophidiophobia is the fear of snakes.

There's a word for that:

Collimate To close one eye while aiming or aligning something.

Nidorosity A burp that smells of undigested roast meat.

Widdly Showy, over-elaborate playing of music, especially with respect to an electric guitar.

Labret A small piece of shell, bone, etc., inserted into or close to the lip as an ornament in some cultures.

Interesting eponyms

The origin of the eponym

bowdlerize

– the removal of sexually offensive words or passages from a written work before publication – is Thomas Bowdler (1754–1825) who published his infamous <u>The Family Shakespeare</u>, with about 10 percent of the material cut or replaced. For example, Lady Macbeth's famous line 'Out, damned spot' became 'Out, crimson spot', and Ophelia's death in <u>Hamlet</u> became an 'accidental drowning'.

The shortest '-ology' is **oology**, the scientific study of eggs.

<u>Paraskevidekatriaphobia</u> is the fear of Friday the 13th.

A committee of vultures

(while resting)

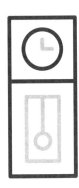

Invented by science fiction:

Time machine
Invented by H G Wells
in his 1895 novella
The Time Machine.

Ask Dr Johnson:

Patron

'One who countenances,
supports or protects.
Commonly a wretch who
supports with insolence,
and is paid with flattery.'

Ten famous malapropisms

1. They misunderestimated me. **George W Bush**

2. He's going up and down like a metronome.
   Ron Pickering

3. Your ambition – is that right – is to abseil across
   the English Channel? **Cilla Black**

4. It will take time to restore chaos and order.
   George W Bush

5. Republicans understand the importance of bondage
   between a mother and child. **Dan Quayle**

6. She's really tough; she's remorseful.
   David Moorcroft

7. We cannot let terrorists and rogue nations hold
   this nation hostile or hold our allies hostile.
   George W Bush

8. And he [Mike Tyson] will have only channel vision.
   Frank Bruno

9. The police are not here to create disorder; they're here
   to preserve disorder. **Richard Daley, former Chicago
   mayor**

10. I am mindful not only of preserving executive
    powers for myself, but for predecessors as well.
    George W Bush

Pediophobia is the fear of dolls.

There's a word for that:

Gynaecomastia The anatomical term for 'man boobs' or 'moobs'.

Mumblecore A subgenre of independent film characterized by naturalistic acting and dialogue, and low-budget production, usually focusing on the personal relationships of millennials.

Canthus The point in the inner or outer corner of the eye where the upper and lower eyelids meet (from the Greek word <u>kanthos</u>).

Erythrophyll The red pigment in leaves, fruits and flowers.

A kettle of vultures

(in flight)

Whatever the weather:

Bombogenesis

Meteorologists use this term to describe when a mid-latitude cyclone intensifies rapidly, and the atmospheric pressure drops at least 24 millibars over 24 hours to create what is known as a 'bomb cyclone'.

Pogonophobia is the fear of beards.

A **fanty-sheeny** is an old English dialect word that means showy or impressive, from <u>fantoccini</u>, an Italian word for puppet show.

<u>Interesting eponyms</u>

The origin of the eponym

boycott

is Captain Charles Cunningham Boycott (1832–97), an English land agent ostracized by his local community in Ireland which was demanding land reform. After many of his employees, including harvesters, withdrew their labour and local shops refused to serve him, 50 Orangemen from County Cavan and County Monaghan harvested the crops, guarded by a regiment of the 19th Royal Hussars and more than 1,000 men of the Royal Irish Constabulary. It cost the British government about £10,000 to harvest the £500 worth of crops.

Ten more phrases Shakespeare 'invented'

1. In a pickle, <u>The Tempest</u>
2. It's Greek to me, <u>Julius Caesar</u>
3. Lie low, <u>Much Ado About Nothing</u>
4. Love is blind, <u>The Merchant of Venice</u>
5. Off with his head, <u>Richard III</u>
6. Pure as the driven snow, <u>Hamlet</u>
7. Seen better days, <u>As You Like It</u>
8. The lady doth protest too much, <u>Hamlet</u>
9. Wear my heart upon my sleeve, <u>Othello</u>
10. Wild goose chase, <u>Romeo and Juliet</u>

<u>Ask Dr Johnson:</u>

Finesse

'An unnecessary word that is creeping into the language.'

<u>Pseudodysphagia</u> is the fear of choking.

Invented by science fiction:

Terraform

The concept first appeared in Jack Williamson's science-fiction story 'Collision Orbit' in 1942.

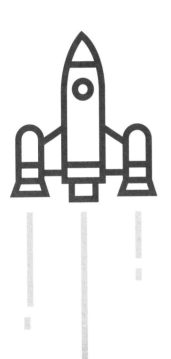

The origin of the sport cricket comes either from the Old French criquet, meaning 'goal, post or stick' or from the Middle Dutch kricke, meaning 'stick' or 'staff'.

The origin of the sport golf comes from its first written appearance in 1457 on a Scottish statute on forbidden games as the Scots word gouf, meaning 'to strike or cuff'.

There's a word for that:

Callomaniac Someone who thinks they are more beautiful than they are.

Erygmatic Causing belching.

Antelucidate To work by candlelight before dawn.

Gowpen The bowl-shaped hollow that is formed when two hands are cupped together (from the Old Norse <u>gaupn</u>)

Pteridophobia is the fear of ferns.

A bazaar of guillemots

Management speak

According to a recent survey of 2,000 business travellers, here are the ten most hated management speak phrases. How many do you still use?

1. Touch base offline
2. Blue-sky thinking
3. Punch a puppy
4. Thought shower
5. Thinking outside the box
6. It's on my radar
7. Close of play
8. Singing from the same hymn sheet
9. Peel the onion
10. To wash its own face

Other repeat offenders that we all hate include 'to circle back', 'drill down', to 'action' something and 'going forward'.

Ask Dr Johnson:

Politician

'A man of artifice; one of deep contrivance.'

To **dismantle** originally meant 'to remove a cloak', from the Old French desmanteler.

Hallux is the anatomical name for your big toe.

Pteromerhanophobia is the fear of flying.

There's a word for that:

Auriphrygiate Fringed with gold.

Callipygian Having shapely buttocks (from the Greek <u>kallos</u> (beauty) and <u>pygē</u> (buttocks).

Upskittle An old Yorkshire dialect term meaning to 'restore to an upright position'.

Glabella The smooth part of the forehead, between and above the eyebrows (from the Latin glaber, meaning 'bald'). Also known as the mesophryon.

A descent of woodpeckers

The opposite of serendipity is zemblanity. The word was introduced in 1998 by William Boyd in his comic bestseller Armadillo: 'zemblanity, the opposite of serendipity, the faculty of making unhappy, unlucky and expected discoveries by design'.

Pupaphobia is the fear of puppets and marionettes.

<u>**Whatever the weather:**</u>

Swullocking
An old English
word meaning
'sultry' or 'humid'.

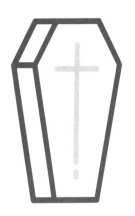

**Taphophilia is the
hobby of visiting
cemeteries.**

Interesting eponyms

The origin of the eponym

maverick

**is Sam Maverick (1803–70), a Texan
politician and land baron who refused
to brand his cattle, which became
known as mavericks.**

Meliorism:
The belief that the world can be made better by human effort.

Invented by science fiction:

Zero gravity
Coined by Jack Binder in a 1938 article for the science-fiction magazine Thrilling Wonder Stories. Arthur C Clarke shortened this to 'zero g' in 1952.

Scoleciphobia is the fear of worms.

There's a word for that:

Cacospectomania A compulsive desire to look at something gruesome, repulsive or horrific.

Antipluvial Protects against the rain.

Acatalepsy The ancient sceptic doctrine that human knowledge is limited to probability and can never achieve certainty.

Dermatoglyphics is the study of fingerprints and skin patterns. It is also the joint longest English **isogram** (word comprised entirely of different letters), tying with **uncopyrightable**.

Spheksophobia is the fear of wasps.

A deceit of lapwings

The longest word in English that appears in the <u>Oxford English Dictionary</u>, is **pneumonoultramicroscopicsilicovolcanoconiosis** which has 45 letters and is a synonym for silicosis, a lung disease caused by inhaling fine ash and sand dust. It was announced at the National Puzzlers' League by its president and inventor, Everett M Smith in 1935. It replaced the 28-letter word 'electrophotomicrographically' in the top spot. The word 'antidisestablishmentarianism' (opposition to the disestablishment of the Church of England) is commonly cited wrongly as the longest word in English, but it doesn't appear in any standard dictionaries.

<u>Ask Dr Johnson</u>:
Kickshaw
'A dish so changed by the cookery that it can scarcely be known.'

Ten most overused and useless English phrases

1. **At the end of the day**
2. **Misuse of 'literally' (e.g. 'I literally died')**
3. **Fairly unique**
4. **I, personally**
5. **At this moment in time**
6. **With all due respect**
7. **Do you know what I mean?**
8. **Thanking you**
9. **110 per cent**
10. **So I turned round and said …**

Taphophobia is the fear of being buried alive by mistake.

Say what?
Contrastive focus reduplication

The next time someone says to you 'I need a <u>drink</u> drink, not a drink', you can tell them that the double construction '<u>drink</u> drink' is an example of what linguists call 'contrastive focus reduplication'. Other examples include 'But do you <u>like</u> like her?' and 'We can go home now, Hodor. Well, maybe not <u>home</u> home, but somewhere that isn't a cave' (from <u>Game of Thrones</u> S6E5). The poem 'After the Funeral' by Billy Collins contains several including '<u>drink</u>-drink', '<u>funeral</u>-funeral' and '<u>elegant</u>-elegant'.

Pooktre is the hobby of growing trees into elaborate shapes, patterns and even furniture. The term was invented by Australian hobbyist couple Peter Cook and Becky Northey.

There's a word for that:

Euneirophrenia A calm and content mood that follows a pleasant night's sleep.

Smeech Dense, foul-smelling or pungent smoke or dust vapour.

Clowking The glugging sound made by pouring liquid from a bottle.

Scotopia Vision in conditions of low light, dark-adapted vision, night vision.

Thalassophobia is the fear of the ocean.

An implausibility of gnus

The Eskimo languages do not contain 400 words for snow. It is a self-regenerating linguistic myth.

<u>Ask Dr Johnson</u>:

Lexicographer

'A writer of dictionaries; a harmless drudge that busies himself in tracing the original, and detailing the signification of words.'

Interesting eponyms

The origin of the eponym

silhouette

is the mid-eighteenth-century French finance minister, Étienne de Silhouette (1709–67) who became unpopular for introducing extreme austerity measures during the Seven Years War. His name became synonymous with doing things 'on the cheap' (à la Silhouette), so the cut paper portraits which were popular at the time were named after him, because they were relatively cheap compared with an oil painting.

The first English dictionary was Richard Mulcaster's Elementarie, a list of 8,000 English words, published in 1582.

Trypophobia is the fear of holes.

Whatever the weather:

Flaggie

Scots have more than 400 words to describe snow. A flaggie is a large snowflake.

The originator of the word **'soccer'** is said to have been an Oxford student named Charles Wredford Brown. In 1863 he was asked if he wanted to take part in a game of 'rugger' (rugby), to which he replied that he preferred 'soccer' (a contraction of the recently created Association Football).

There's a word for that:

Historiaster An inferior or mediocre historian.

Pulveratrix A bird that grooms its feathers by driving dust into the plumage and shaking it out.

Purlicue In northern England, it is the word for the space between the forefinger and thumb. It also means a summary given at the end of a sermon or address, and it has an obsolete meaning in Scotland as a flourish at the end of a pen stroke.

Frenulum A small ligament or fold of membrane that restricts movement between body parts (from the Latin fraenum, meaning 'bridle'). The most obvious example is the fold on the underside of the tongue.

Thrapple Throat, windpipe.

Venustraphobia **is the fear of beautiful women.**